In the Dark Woods

Written by Hawys Morgan

Illustrated by Marina Perez Luque

Collins

The moon lights up the woods.

Hear the fox bark.

Look up high in this oak.

Hush! Owls hoot.

Toads soak in the pool.

otter

The air feels cool.

Look in the marsh.

Eels coil up in the weeds.

We see a herd.

We hear a moan.

hurt foot

11

Mum is a vet.

The hoof gets better.

The woods

 Review: After reading

Use your assessment from hearing the children read to choose any GPCs, words or tricky words that need additional practice.

Read 1: Decoding

- Focus on the words in which two or three letters make one sound.
- Ask the children to find the words ending in "s". Tell them the "s" can make the sound /z/ or /s/ at the end of words. Ask them to read the words thinking carefully about the sound the "s" is making.

Read 2: Prosody

- Choose two double page spreads and model reading with expression to the children. Ask the children to have a go at reading the same pages with expression.
- Discuss how you point to the object that is labelled as you read the label.
- Show children how you read with a whisper to add to the atmosphere.

Read 3: Comprehension

- Turn to pages 14 and 15 and ask the children to describe each creature they saw in the woods, where it was and what it did.
- For every question ask the children how they know the answer. Ask:
  - What three things do the characters hear in the woods? (*bark of a fox; hoot of owls; moan of a deer*)
  - What two things do they see in the water? (*toads and eels*)
  - Why was the deer moaning? (*it had hurt its hoof*)